# ROY KEANE

Andy Croft

Published in association with The Basic Skills Agency

Hodder

The Publishers would like to thank the following for permission to reproduce copyright material:

**Photo credits**
p.3 © Tony Harris/PA Photos; p.7 © Phil O'Brien/EMPICS; p.11 © John Peters/ Manchester United via Getty Images; p.14 © David Cannon/Getty Images; p.17 © Laurence Griffiths/EMPICS; p.21 © Magi Haroun/EMPICS; p.24 © Clive Brunskill/Getty Images.

Orders: please contact Bookpoint Ltd, 130 Milton Park, Abingdon, Oxon OX14 4SB. Telephone (44) 01235 827720. Fax: (44) 01235 400454. Lines are open from 9.00–6.00, Monday to Saturday, with a 24-hour message answering service. You can also order through our website www.hoddereducation.co.uk

Copyright © Andy Croft 2003, 2005
Second Edition. First published in 2003 by
Hodder Murray, a member of the Hodder Headline Group
338 Euston Road
London NW1 3BH

Impression number   10 9 8 7 6 5 4 3 2 1
Year                          2010  2009  2008  2007 2006 2005

Cover photo © Chris Trotman/New Sport/Corbis
Typeset in 14pt Palatino by SX Composing DTP, Rayleigh, Essex.
Printed in Great Britain by CPI Bath.

A catalogue record for this title is available from the British Library

ISBN-10 0 340 90077 6
ISBN-13 978 0 340 90077 2

# Contents

# 1 The Birth of a Legend

Roy Maurice Keane
was born on 10 August 1971
in the city of Cork
in the Irish Republic.

He was the fourth of five children.
His dad worked in a local textile factory.
The family didn't have much money.
They were a football-mad family.
The rest of the family
supported Manchester United.
Roy supported Spurs.

Roy Keane went to St John's Primary School
and Mayfield Community School.

He played football all the time.
Before school, at dinnertime,
after school, every weekend.
Because he was small for his age,
he only played twice for his junior school team.

He joined a local junior team when he was nine.
They were called Rockmount AFC.
He played for the Under-10s,
the Under-11s and the Under-12s.
And he was still only nine!
At the end of his first season,
Rockmount voted Roy Keane Player of the Year.
Rockmount won the League and Cup Double
for the next six seasons.
They won every game for four years!

Roy Keane.

Roy Keane tried to build up his strength.
He tried Gaelic football,
a game played mainly in Ireland.
He even tried boxing.

Roy Keane left school at 15.
He failed his exams.
He couldn't get a job.
He just wanted to play football.
He wrote to English League clubs asking for a trial.
No one was interested.
He didn't even bother writing to
Manchester United.
He thought they were too good for him!

# 2 Forest

When Roy was 17,
he joined a local team
called Cobh Ramblers.
A scout from Nottingham Forest
soon spotted him playing for them.
Forest asked him to go for a trial for the club.

The Forest manager
was the famous Brian Clough.
He knew Roy Keane was special.
Forest bought him for £47,000
in May 1990.

At first Roy was homesick.
He missed his family back in Ireland.
Clough always called him the Irishman.

He played in an Under-21 competition in Holland
and scored two goals.
Soon he was in the Forest reserve team.
He scored two goals in his first game.

A few weeks later,
he was in the first team against Liverpool.
In the next match,
he set up a goal against Southampton.
Brian Clough was so pleased
that he kissed him in front of all the fans!
He scored his first League goal for Forest
against Sheffield United.

Keane receives the Barclays Young Player of the
Month award at Nottingham Forest, 1991.

Roy Keane played 49 games for Forest
in his first season.
In 1991, he helped them reach
the FA Cup Final,
but they lost to Spurs,
the team he'd supported as a boy.

The next season he scored against Spurs
to take Forest to the League Cup Final.
They lost 1–0 to Manchester United in the final.
He was voted Young Eagle of the Year
and Player of the Year at Forest.

In three seasons at Nottingham Forest,
Roy Keane played 153 games.

# 3 Keano

Roy Keane is a very special player.
He doesn't score many goals.
He doesn't dribble.
He doesn't cross the ball.
But he's one of the best midfield players
in the world.

He may be small,
but he wins the ball.
He tackles hard.
He isn't afraid.
He passes well.

He jumps high.
He can head the ball.
He sets up goals.
He makes late runs into the box
and scores important goals.
He runs and runs
and runs and runs,
and never stops.

Roy Keane never gives up.
Roy Keane wants to win.

This also means he gets a lot of injuries.
It means he sometimes gets in trouble with referees.

Roy Keane and Robbie Savage, Barclays
Premiership match between Birmingham City
and Manchester United, 2004.

# 4 Manchester United 1

At the end of 1992–3, Forest were relegated.
Manchester United wanted to buy Roy Keane.
So did Arsenal and Blackburn.
United manager Alex Ferguson
had already tried to buy him twice.
This time Ferguson got his man.

In July 1993, Roy Keane
joined Manchester United
for £3.75 million.
It was a British record.
And he was still only 21 years old.

Keane played his first game for United
in the Charity Shield against Arsenal.
In his first League game,
he crossed the ball for Ryan Giggs to score.
In his first game at Old Trafford,
United's home ground,
he scored two goals against Sheffield United.
A few weeks later,
he scored two goals in the Champions' League.

In the 1992–3 season, Roy Keane helped United
win the FA Cup and League Double.
They had never won both in the same season.

In 1994, he became Britain's youngest
football millionaire.

Manchester United celebrate a goal in the 1994
FA Cup Final.

# 5 World Cup USA

Roy Keane was soon a regular in the Ireland team.

He first played for Ireland
in 1991 against Chile.
In 1994, he helped his home country
reach the World Cup
in the USA.

Ireland beat Italy 1–0.
They lost 1–2 to Mexico.
They drew 0–0 with Norway.
They drew 0–0 with Holland.
Then they were out of the World Cup.

Roy Keane wasn't happy.
He didn't like Ireland's tactics.
The Ireland manager, Jack Charlton,
told the players to kick the ball up the pitch.
Roy Keane didn't want to.
He wanted to play a passing game.

Keane was far from happy.
But he was still voted
the best Irish player in the World Cup.

Keane and Eric Cantona celebrate winning the
Double in 1996.

# 6 Manchester United 2

In 1996, United won the Double again.
When Eric Cantona retired in 1997,
Roy Keane became United captain.

He missed the 1997–8 season
because of a knee injury.
United won nothing that year.

When he came back from injury,
United won the Double again in 1999.
Only three other players in history
have won both the League and FA Cup
three times.

Manchester United was the best team in Britain.
Roy Keane wanted them
to be the best team in Europe.
In 1998, he took them to the
Champions' League final.
He scored in the semi-final
against Juventus.
United went on to beat Bayern Munich
in the final.
Roy Keane couldn't play in the match
because he had a yellow card.
He was banned from playing.

In 1999, he was voted
Manchester United Player of the Year.

In 2000, United were champions again.
And again in 2001.
Roy Keane has helped United
win the League seven times.

In 12 seasons,
Roy Keane has played
403 games for Manchester United
and scored 47 goals.

In 2000, he was voted FA Player of the Year.
In 2001, United fans voted him
seventh best United player in history.
Alex Ferguson says Keane is perhaps
the best United player of all time.

Roy Keane holding the trophy for Manchester United Player of the Year 1998–9 with Sandy Busby (son of Sir Matt Busby).

# 7 Keano Says

The following are quotes from Roy Keane himself.

– I love winning.
– I would be just as happy without my money.
– Roy Keane is not a great player.
– The only thing that goes with the flow is dead fish.
– It is the lows that keep me going.
– Players need to stand up and be counted.
– Good players don't necessarily make good teams.
– Work as hard as you can
    and eventually you will get your rewards.
– There are so many players better than me
    who haven't made it.
– Getting to major finals is what it is all about.
– Fail to prepare, prepare to fail.
– Some people are sheep. I am a wolf.

# 8 The Man

Roy Keane is one of the most famous footballers
in the world.
He is captain of the most famous football club
in the world.

He has played 59 times for his country.
He is recognised everywhere he goes.
United fans love Keano.

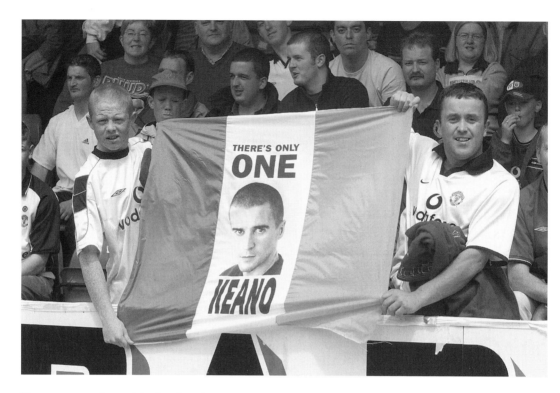

Keano: popular with the fans!

He may be a football 'hard man',
but Roy Keane is also a very private person.
Roy Keane does a lot of work for charity.
He is a quiet, shy man.
He likes staying at home with his family.

Is he a hard man
or a family man?
Is he a saint or a sinner?
One thing is certain:
Roy Keane is a winner,
and a fantastic football player.

# 9 Keano Quiz

1     In which country was Roy Keane born?

2     What other sports did Roy Keane play as a boy?

3     Which team did Roy Keane support when he was a boy?

4     How much did Nottingham Forest pay for Roy Keane?

5     Against which country did Roy Keane win his first cap for Ireland?

6     How many games did Roy Keane play for Nottingham Forest?

7     How much money did Manchester United pay for Roy Keane?

8    How many times has Roy Keane
     won the Premiership?

9    How many times has Roy Keane
     won the Double?

10   Against which club did Roy Keane score
     his first goal for Manchester United?